Green Day

Insomniac

© 1996 WARNER BROS. PUBLICATIONS
All Rights Reserved

Transcribers: Bill La Fleur and Eli Simpson
Project Manager: Aaron Stang
Music Editor: Colgan Bryan
Book Art Design: Joseph Klucar

Album Art Collage: Winston Smith
Album Art Direction: Dirk Walter
Album Art Designer: David Harlan

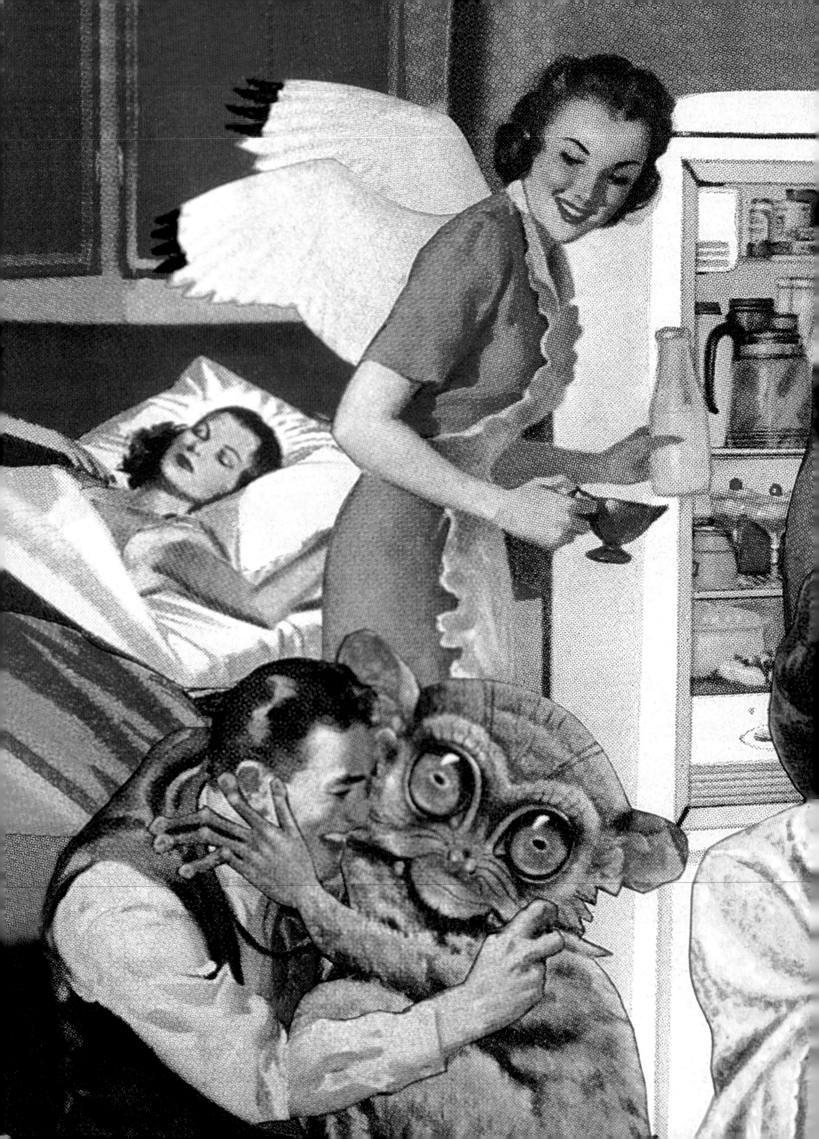

BRAT

Lyrics by BILLIE JOE
Music by BILLIE JOE and GREEN DAY

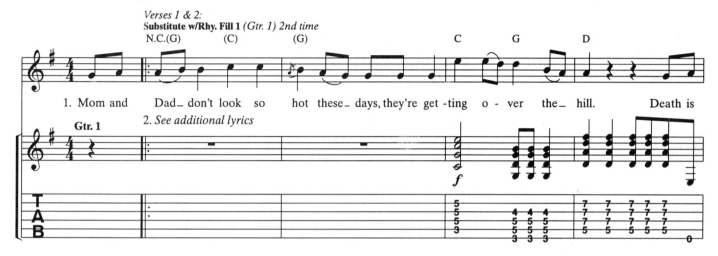

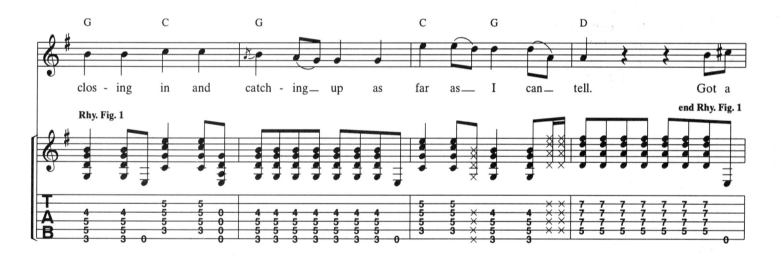

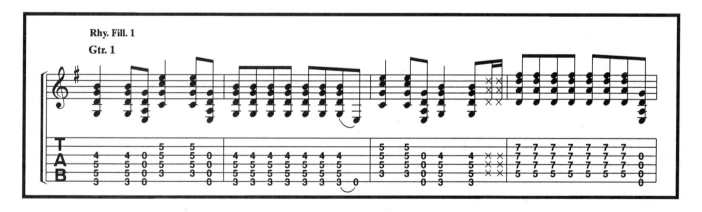

Brat - 3 - 1
PG9556

6

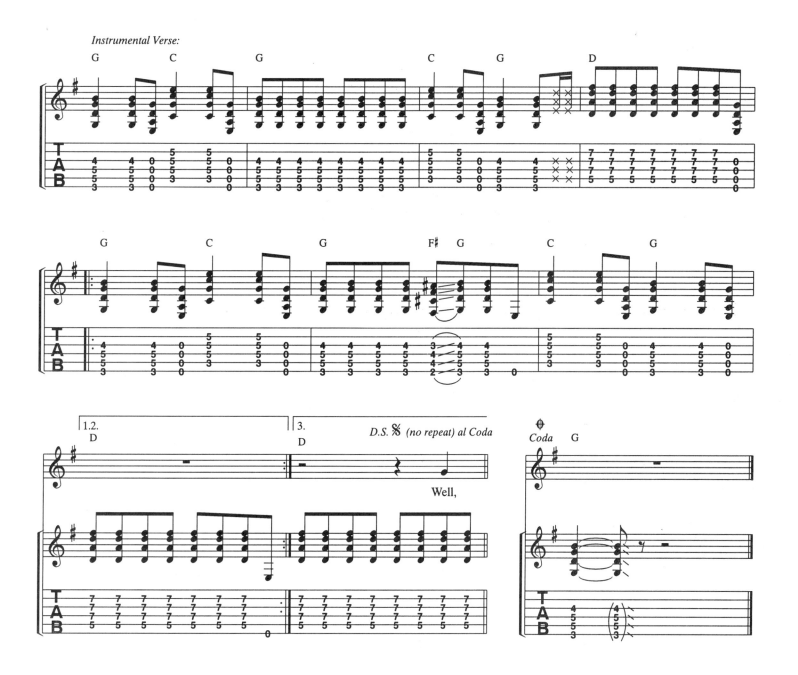

Verse 2:
Crow's feet and rot are setting in,
And time is running out.
My parent's income interest rate
Is gaining higher clout.
I'm a snot-nosed slob without a job
And I know I damn well should.
Mom and Dad don't look so hot these days
But my future's looking good.

ARMATAGE SHANKS

Lyrics by BILLIE JOE
Music by BILLIE JOE and GREEN DAY

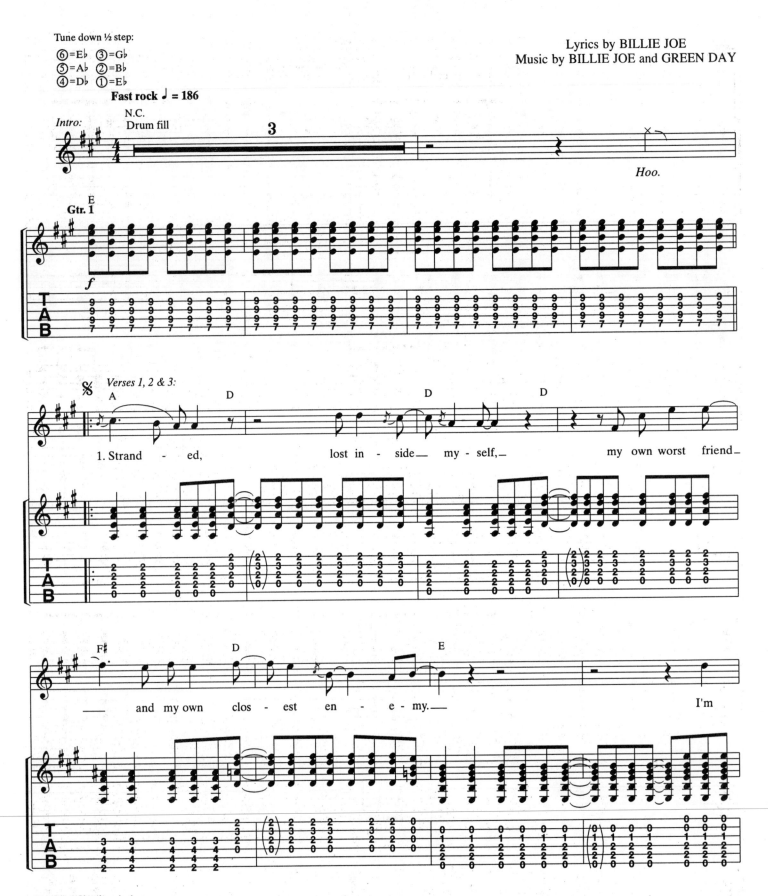

Armatage Shanks - 4 - 1
PG9556

*Sung 1st time only.

10

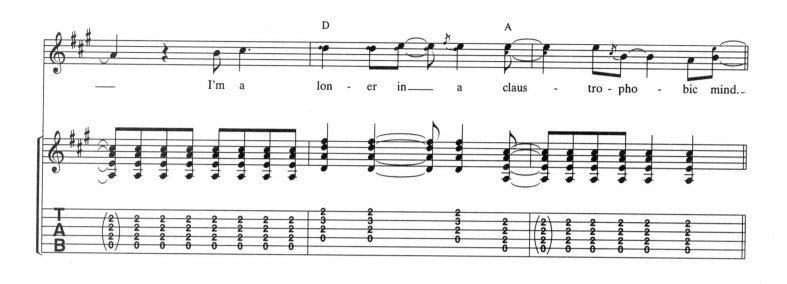

I'm a lon - er in___ a claus - tro - pho - bic mind.__

Outro:

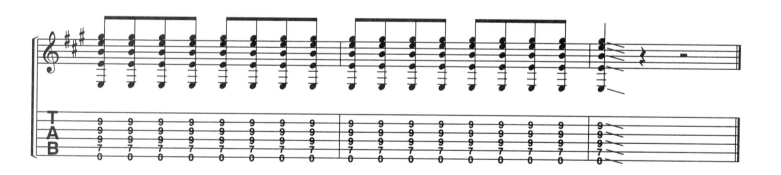

Verse 2:
Elected, the rejected.
I perfect the science of the idiot.
No meaning and no healing.
Self - loathing freak and introverted deviot.
(To Chorus:)

Verse 3:
Stranded, lost inside myself.
My own worst friend and my own closest enemy.
Elected, the rejected.
I perfect the science of the idiot.
(To Chorus:)

STUCK WITH ME

Lyrics by BILLIE JOE
Music by BILLIE JOE and GREEN DAY

Stuck With Me - 4 - 1
PG9556

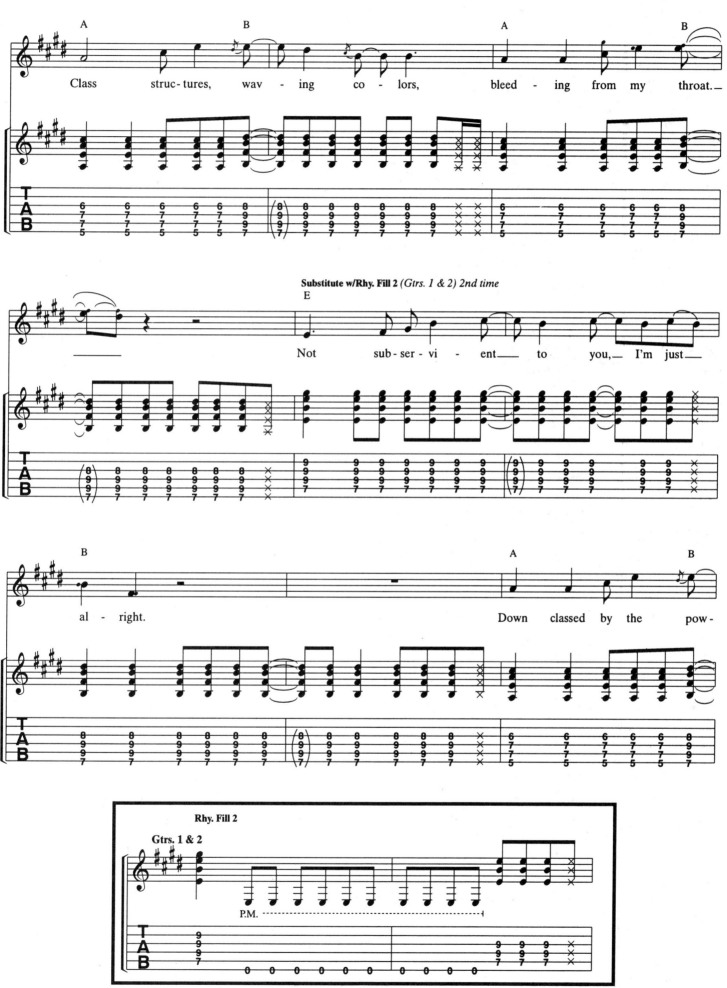

14

ers that be, give me loss of hope.

Chorus:
Cast out, bur - ied in a hole.

Rhy. Fig. 1 end Rhy. Fig. 1

w/Rhy. Fig. 1 *(Gtrs. 1 & 2) 2 times*

Struck down, forc - ing me to fall.

De - stroyed, giv - ing up the fight. Well, I

1.3. *Fine*

know I'm not al - right.

Verse 2:
What's my price and will you pay it
If it's alright?
Take it from my dignity and
Waste it 'til it's dead.
Throw me back into the gutter
'Cause it's alright.
Find another pleasure fucker,
Drag them down to hell.

GEEK STINK BREATH

All Gtrs. tune down ½ step:

⑥=E♭ ③=G♭
⑤=A♭ ②=B♭
④=D♭ ①=E♭

Lyrics by BILLIE JOE
Music by BILLIE JOE and GREEN DAY

*w/vocal "croak" effect (1st time).

1. (I'm) on a mis-sion. I made my de-ci-sion, lead a path of self-de-struc-tion.

2.3. See additional lyrics

(A) slow pro-gres-sion, kill-ing my com-plex-ion and it's

Geek Stink Breath - 3 - 1
PG9556

Verse 2:
Every hour my blood is turning sour
And my pulse is beating out of time.
I found a treasure filled with sick pleasure
And it sits on a thin, white line.
(To Pre-Chorus:)

Verse 3:
I'm on a mission.
I got no decision,
Like a cripple running the rat race.
Wish in one hand and shit in the other,
And see which one gets filled first.
(To Pre-Chorus:)

NO PRIDE

Lyrics by BILLIE JOE
Music by BILLIE JOE and GREEN DAY

1. Well, I am just a mutt,
(Cont. in slashes)
2. See additional lyrics

and no-where is my home, where dig-

ni-ty's a land-mine in the school of lost hope.

I've pan-han-dled for life 'cause I'm not

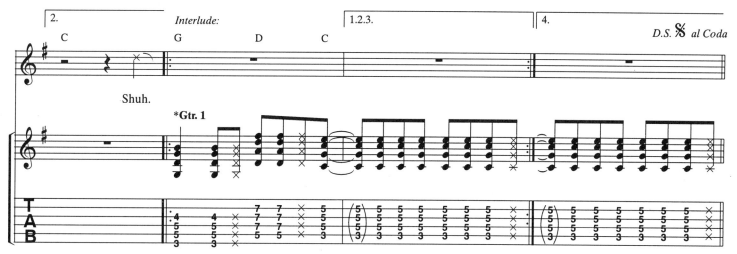

*Gtr. 1 double tracked at this point.

Verse 2:
Well, sects of disconnection
And traditions of lost faith.
No culture's worth a stream of piss
Or a bullet in my face.
To hell with unity,
Separation's gonna kill us all.
Torn to shreds and disjointed
Before the final fall.

BAB'S UVULA WHO?

Lyrics by BILLIE JOE
Music by BILLIE JOE and GREEN DAY

Tune down ½ step:

⑥=E♭ ③=G♭
⑤=A♭ ②=B♭
④=D♭ ①=E♭

Fast rock ♩ = 187

Intro:

1. I've got a knack for fuck-ing ev'-ry-thing up, ___
2. *See additional lyrics*

my tem-per flies and I get my-self all wound up.

My fuse is short and my blood pres-sure is high, ___

Bab's Uvula Who? - 4 - 1
PG9556

24

Pet - u - lance and ir - ri - ta - tion set in,____

D.S. 𝄋 al Coda

I throw a tan - trum and I get my - self all wound up.

Coda   w/Rhy. Fig. 2 *(Gtr. 1)*

What can I say, I'm 'fraid I'm all wound up.

Verse 2:

Chip on my shoulder and a leech on my back,
Stuck in a rut and I get myself all wound up.
Killed my composure and it will never come back,
Loss of control and I get myself all wound up.
Blown out of proportion again,
My temper snaps and I get myself all wound up.
Spontaneous combustion, panic attack,
I slipped a gear and I get myself all wound up.

Chorus 2:

I hate myself and I'm all wound up.
What can I say, I'm afraid I'm all wound up.
I hate myself and I'm all wound up.
I like myself and I'm all wound up.

Chorus 3:

I hate myself and I'm all wound up.
Loss of control and I'm all wound up.
What can I say, I'm afraid I'm all wound up.

86

Lyrics by BILLIE JOE
Music by BILLIE JOE and GREEN DAY

86 - 4 - 1
PG9556

*Sung 1st time only, vocal tacet on repeats.

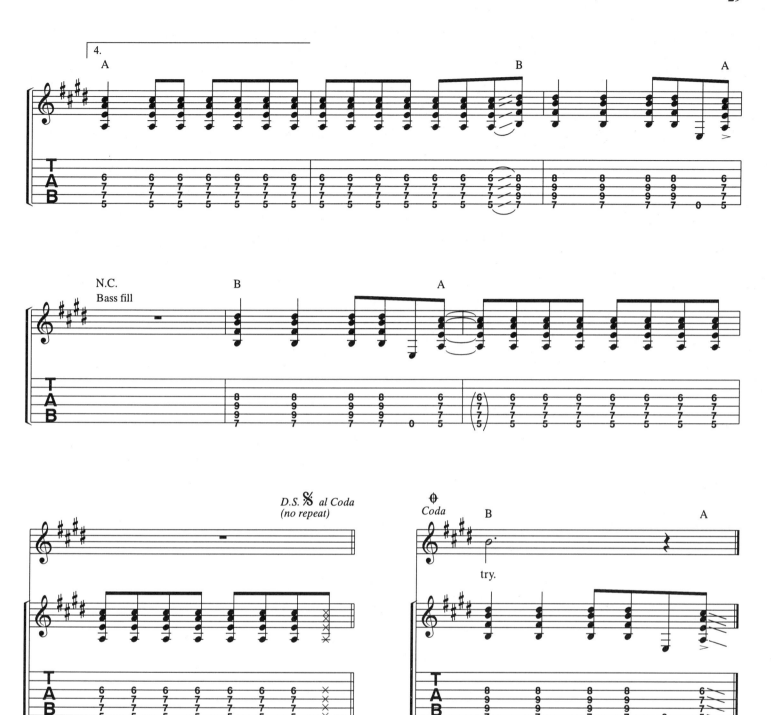

Verse 2:
Exit out the back
And never show your head around again.
Purchase your ticket
And quickly take the last train out of town.

Armatage Shanks

Stranded... lost inside myself
My own worst friend
My own closest enemy
Branded... Maladjusted

Never trusted anyone
Let alone myself
I must insist
On being a pessimist

I'm a loner in a catastrophic mind
Elected the rejected
I perfected the science of the idiot

No meaning... no healing
Self loathing freak and introverted
Deviot

Brat

Mom and Dad don't look so hot these days
They're getting over the hill
Death is closing in and catching up
As far as I can tell
Got a plan of action and cold blood
And it smells of defiance
I'll just wait for Mom and Dad to die
And get my inheritance

Now I want more
'Cause I'm getting bored
And I'm going nowhere fast

I was once filled with doubt
Now it's all figured out
Nothing good can last
Crows feet and rot are setting in
And time is running out
My parent's income interest rate
Is gaining higher clout

I'm a snot nosed slob
Without a job
And I know I damn well should

Mom and Dad don't look so hot these days
But my future's looking good

Stuck With Me

I'm not part of your elite
I'm just alright
Class structure waving colors
Bleeding from my throat
Not subservient to you I'm just alright
Down classed by the powers that be
Give me loss of hope

Cast out... Buried in a hole
Struck down... forcing me to fall
Destroyed... giving up the fight

I know I'm not alright
What's my price and will you pay it
If it's alright?
Take it from my dignity
Waste it until it's dead
Throw me back into the gutter
'Cause it's alright

Find another pleasure fucker
Drag them down to hell

Jaded

Somebody keep my balance
I think I'm falling off
Into a state of regression
The expiration date
Rapidly coming up
It's leaving me behind to fade
Always move forward
Going "straight" will get you nowhere
There is no progress
Evolution killed it all
I found my place in nowhere
I'm taking one step sideways
Leading with my crutch
Got a fucked up equilibrium
Count down from 9 to 5
Hooray! We're gonna die!
Blessed into our extirpation

86

What brings you around?
Did you lose something the last time you were here?
You'll never find it now

It's buried deep with your identity
So stand aside and let the next one pass
Don't let the door kick you in the ass

There's no return from 86
Don't ever try

Exit out the back
And never show your head around again
Purchase your ticket and
Quickly take the last train
Out of town

Panic Song

Ready for a cheap escape
Or the brink of self destruction
Widespread panic
Broken glass inside my head
Bleeding down these thoughts of
Anguish... mass confusion
The world is a sick machine
Bleeding a mass of shit
With such a desolate conclusion
Fill the vOid with... I don't care
There's a plague inside of me
Eating at my disposition
Nothing's left
Torn out of reality
Into a state of no opinion
Limp with hate

No pride

I'm just a mutt
And nowhere is my home
Where dignity's a land mine
In the school of lost hope

I've panhandled for life because
I'm not afraid to beg
Hand me down your lost and founds
You better Of second hand regret
Or you're gonna
You better digest your values
Because they turn to shit

Honor's gonna knock you down
Before your chance to stand up and fight
I know I'm not the one
I got no pride
Sects of disconnection
And traditions of lost faith
No culture's worth a stream of piss
Or a bullet in my face

To hell with unity
Separation's gonna kill us all
Torn to shreds and disjointed
Before the final fall

Bab's Uvula Who?

I've got a knack for fucking everything up
My temper flies and I get myself all wound up
My fuse is short and my blood pressure is high
I lose control and I get myself all wound up
Tension mounts and I fly off the wall all wound up
I self-destruct and I get myself all wound up
Petulance and irritation sets in all wound up
I throw a tantrum and I get myself all wound up
Stuck in a rut and I get myself all wound up
I've got a chip on my shoulder and a leech on my back
Killed my composure and it will never come back
Loss of control and I get myself all wound up
Blown out of proportion again all wound up
My temper snaps and I get myself all wound up
Spontaneous combustion all wound up
Panic attack
I slipped a gear and I get myself all wound up

Westbound Sign

Boxed up
All of her favorite things
Sold the rest at a rainy yard sale
Big plans and leaving friends and
A westbound sign
Weighed out
Her choices on a scale
Prevailing nothing made sense
Just transportation and a
Blank decision... She's taking off
No time and no copping out
She's burning daylight and petrol
Blacked out the rearview mirror
Heading westward or
Strung out
Or confusion road
And ten minute nervous breakdowns
Xanex a beer for thought
And she determined... She's taking off
Is it salvation?
Or an escape from discontent?
Will she find her name
In the California cement?
Punched out of the grind
That punched her one too many times...
Is tragedy 2000 miles away?
She's taking
off

Tight Wad Hill

Cheapskate on the hill
A thrill seeker making deals
Sugar city urchin wasting time
Town of lunatics

Begging for another fix
Turning tricks for speedballs
One more night
Making your rounds once again
Turning up empty handed

Bumming a ride
Burning daylight
Last up at dawn... tight wad hill
Drugstore hooligan
Another white trash marrequir
On display to rot up on the hill
Living out a life
But having the time of his life
Hating every minute of his existence

Geek Stink Breath

I'm on a mission
I made my decision
To lead a path of self-destruction
A slow progression
Killing my complexion
And it's rotting out my teeth

I'm on a roll
No self control
I'm blowing off steam with
Meth Amphetamine
Don't know what I want
That's all that I've got
And I'm picking scabs off my face
Every hour my blood is turning sour

And my pulse is beating out of time

I found a treasure
Filled with sick pleasure
And it sits on a thick white line
I'm on a mission
I got no decision like a cripple
Running the rat race
Wish in one hand and shit in the other
And see which one gets filled first

Walking Contradiction

Do as I say not as I do because
The shit so deep you can't run away
I beg to differ on the contrary
I agree with every word that you say
Talk is cheap and lies are expensive
My wallet's fat and so is my head
Hit and run and then I'll hit you again
I'm a smart-ass but I'm playing dumb.
Standards set and broken all the time
Control the chaos behind a gun
Call it as I see it even if
I was born deaf, blind and dumb
Losers winning big on the lottery
Rehab rejects still sniffing glue
Constant refutation with myself
I'm a victim of a catch 22
I have no belief
But I believe
I'm a walking contradiction
And I ain't got no right

Brain Stew

I'm having trouble trying to sleep
I'm counting sheep but running out
As time ticks by
And still I try
No rest for crosstops in my mind
On my own... here we go

My eyes feel like they're going to bleed
Dried up and bulging out my skull
My mouth is dry
My face is numb
Fucked up and spun out in my room

On my own... here we go
My mind is set on overdrive

The clock is laughing in my face
A crooked spine
My sense dulled
Passed the point of delirium

On my own... here we go

Stuart And The Ave.

Standing on the corner of
Stuart and the Ave.
Ripping up my transfer
And a photograph of you
You're a blur of my dead past and rotting existence
As I stand laughing on the corner of insignificance
Destiny is dead

In the hands of bad luck
Before it might have made some sense
But now it's all fucked up
Seasons change as well as minds
And I'm a two-faced clown

You're mommy's little nightmare
Driving daddy's car around
I'm beat down and half brain dead
The long lost king of fools
I may be dumb
But I'm not stupid enough to stay with you

All songs except "Panic Song":
Lyrics by Billie Joe
Music by Billie Joe and Green Day

Panic Song:
Lyrics by Mike Dirnt and Billie Joe
Music by Billie Joe and Green Day

PANIC SONG

Lyrics by MIKE DIRNT and BILLIE JOE
Music by BILLIE JOE and GREEN DAY

Verse 4:
Torn out of reality
Into a state of no opinion.
Limp with hate.

STUART AND THE AVE.

Lyrics by BILLIE JOE
Music by BILLIE JOE and GREEN DAY

Verse 2:
Seasons change as well as minds,
And I'm a two-faced clown.
You're mommy's little nightmare,
Driving daddy's car around.
I'm beat down and half brain dead,
The long lost king of fools.
I may be dumb, but I'm not stupid
Enough to stay with you.

BRAIN STEW

Lyrics by BILLIE JOE
Music by BILLIE JOE and GREEN DAY

*Vib. applies to fretted notes only (throughout).

Verse 2:
My eyes feel like they're going to bleed,
Dried up and bulging out my skull.
My mouth is dry,
My face is numb.
Fucked up and spun out in my room.

Verse 3:
My mind is set on overdrive.
The clock is laughing in my face.
A crooked spine,
My sense is dulled.
Passed the point of delirium.

JADED

Lyrics by BILLIE JOE
Music by BILLIE JOE and GREEN DAY

Jaded - 2 - 1
PG9556

There is no prog - ress.__ Ev - o - lu - tion killed it

all. I found my place in no - where.__

You're no - where.__ You're no -

where.

Verse 2:
I'm taking one step sideways,
Leading with my crutch.
Got a fucked up equilibrium.
Count down from nine to five.
Hooray! We're gonna die,
Blessed into our extinction.

WESTBOUND SIGN

Lyrics by BILLIE JOE
Music by BILLIE JOE and GREEN DAY

Verse 2:
No time and no copping out.
She's burning daylight and petrol.
Blacked out the rearview mirror,
Heading westward on.
Strung out on confusion road,
And ten minute nervous breakdowns.
Xanex, a beer for thought,
And she's determined.
(To Chorus:)

TIGHT WAD HILL

Lyrics by BILLIE JOE
Music by BILLIE JOE and GREEN DAY

Tight Wad Hill - 2 - 1
PG9556

47

Verse 2:
Drugstore hooligan,
Another white trash mannequin,
On display to rot up on the hill.
Living out a lie
But having the time of his life,
Hating every minute of his existence.

Tight Wad Hill - 2 - 2
PG9556

WALKING CONTRADICTION

All gtrs. tune down 1/2 step:

⑥=Eb ③=Gb
⑤=Ab ②=Bb
④=Db ①=Eb

Lyrics by BILLIE JOE
Music by BILLIE JOE and GREEN DAY

Moderately fast ♩ = 132
Intro:

Gtrs. 1 & 2   A5

f P.M.

Faster ♩ = 152
Verse:

D   G5   A5   D   G5   A5

1. 3. Do as I say, not— as I do be-cause the shit's so deep can you run a-way. I
2. *See additional lyrics*

Rhy. Fig. 1   end Rhy. Fig. 1

w/Rhy. Fig. 1 *(Gtrs. 1 & 2) 4 times*

D   G5   A5   D   G5   A5

beg to dif-fer, on— the con-tra-ry, I a-gree with ev-'ry word— that you say.

D   G5   A5   D   G5   A5

Talk is cheap and lies— are ex-pen-sive, my wal-let's fat and so— is my head.

D   G5   A5   D   G5   A5

Hit and run, and then— I'll hit you a-gain, a smart ass but— I'm— play-ing dumb.

1.

D   G5   A5   D   G5   A5

Walking Contradiction - 3 - 1
PG9556

Verse 2:
Standards set and broken all the time,
Control the chaos behind a gun.
Call it as I see it, even if
I was born deaf, blind and dumb.
Losers winning big on the lottery,
Rehab rejects still sniffing glue.
Constant refutation with myself,
I'm a victim of a catch 22.

GUITAR TAB GLOSSARY **

TABLATURE EXPLANATION

READING TABLATURE: Tablature illustrates the six strings of the guitar. Notes and chords are indicated by the placement of fret numbers on a given string(s).

String ⑥, 3rd Fret   *String ① 12th Fret*   A "C" Chord   C Chord Arpeggiated
String ① 13th Fret

BENDING NOTES

HALF STEP: Play the note and bend string one half step.*

WHOLE STEP: Play the note and bend string one whole step.

WHOLE STEP AND A HALF: Play the note and bend string a whole step and a half.

SLIGHT BEND (Microtone): Play the note and bend string slightly to the equivalent of half a fret.

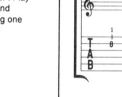

PREBEND (Ghost Bend): Bend to the specified note, before the string is picked.

PREBEND AND RELEASE: Bend the string, play it, then release to the original note.

REVERSE BEND: Play the already-bent string, then immediately drop it down to the fretted note.

BEND AND RELEASE: Play the note and gradually bend to the next pitch, then release to the original note. Only the first note is attacked.

*A half step is the smallest interval in Western music; it is equal to one fret. A whole step equals two frets.

UNISON BEND: Play both notes and immediately bend the lower note to the same pitch as the higher note.

DOUBLE NOTE BEND: Play both notes and immediately bend both strings simultaneously.

BENDS INVOLVING MORE THAN ONE STRING: Play the note and bend string while playing an additional note (or notes) on another string(s). Upon release, relieve pressure from additional note(s), causing original note to sound alone.

BENDS INVOLVING STATIONARY NOTES: Play notes and bend lower pitch, then hold until release begins (indicated at the point where line becomes solid).

TREMOLO BAR

SPECIFIED INTERVAL: The pitch of a note or chord is lowered to a specified interval and then may or may not return to the original pitch. The activity of the tremolo bar is graphically represented by peaks and valleys.

UN-SPECIFIED INTERVAL: The pitch of a note or a chord is lowered to an unspecified interval.

HARMONICS

NATURAL HARMONIC: A finger of the fret hand lightly touches the note or notes indicated in the tab and is played by the pick hand.

ARTIFICIAL HARMONIC: The first tab number is fretted, then the pick hand produces the harmonic by using a finger to lightly touch the same string at the second tab number (in parenthesis) and is then picked by another finger.

ARTIFICIAL "PINCH" HARMONIC: A note is fretted as indicated by the tab, then the pick hand produces the harmonic by squeezing the pick firmly while using the tip of the index finger in the pick attack. If parenthesis are found around the fretted note, it does not sound. No parenthesis means both the fretted note and A.H. are heard simultaneously.

**By Kenn Chipkin and Aaron Stang

RHYTHM SLASHES

STRUM INDICATIONS: Strum with indicated rhythm.

The chord voicings are found on the first page of the transcription underneath the song title.

INDICATING SINGLE NOTES USING RHYTHM SLASHES: Very often single notes are incorporated into a rhythm part. The note name is indicated above the rhythm slash with a fret number and a string indication.

ARTICULATIONS

HAMMER ON: Play lower note, then "hammer on" to higher note with another finger. Only the first note is attacked.

LEFT HAND HAMMER: Hammer on the first note played on each string with the left hand.

PULL OFF: Play higher note, then "pull off" to lower note with another finger. Only the first note is attacked.

FRET-BOARD TAPPING: "Tap" onto the note indicated by + with a finger of the pick hand, then pull off to the following note held by the fret hand.

TAP SLIDE: Same as fretboard tapping, but the tapped note is slid randomly up the fretboard, then pulled off to the following note.

BEND AND TAP TECHNIQUE: Play note and bend to specified interval. While holding bend, tap onto note indicated.

LEGATO SLIDE: Play note and slide to the following note. (Only first note is attacked).

LONG GLISSANDO: Play note and slide in specified direction for the full value of the note.

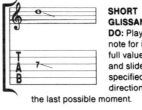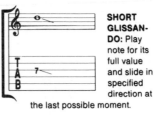

SHORT GLISSANDO: Play note for its full value and slide in specified direction at the last possible moment.

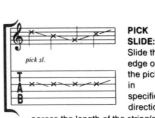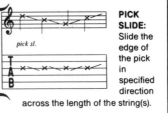

PICK SLIDE: Slide the edge of the pick in specified direction across the length of the string(s).

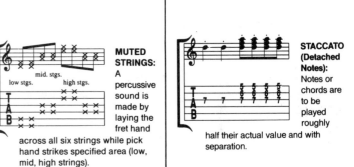

MUTED STRINGS: A percussive sound is made by laying the fret hand across all six strings while pick hand strikes specified area (low, mid, high strings).

PALM MUTE: The note or notes are muted by the palm of the pick hand by lightly touching the string(s) near the bridge.

TREMOLO PICKING: The note or notes are picked as fast as possible.

TRILL: Hammer on and pull off consecutively and as fast as possible between the original note and the grace note.

ACCENT: Notes or chords are to be played with added emphasis.

STACCATO (Detached Notes): Notes or chords are to be played roughly half their actual value and with separation.

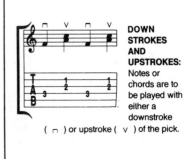

DOWN STROKES AND UPSTROKES: Notes or chords are to be played with either a downstroke (⊓) or upstroke (∨) of the pick.

VIBRATO: The pitch of a note is varied by a rapid shaking of the fret hand finger, wrist, and forearm.

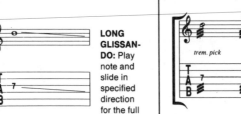